Henry Meets a Honey Bee

Written and Illustrated by:
Justin Ruger
Published and Distributed by:
Hippie Chick Apiary

Henry Meets a Honey Bee by Hippie Chick Apiary

Published in honor of Shirley Chaney Lawrence on October 09, 2021, to celebrate what would have been her 60th birthday. Love and Miss you!

I dedicate this book to three people who have made a major difference in my life.

First, I dedicate this to my second mother, Shirley Chaney Lawrence. I love you more than words can describe. Your smile always lit up my heart and made me feel safe no matter what I was going through. Losing you to COVID is one of the hardest things I've ever had to deal with. I know you are by my side, and you will forever be in my heart and on my mind. You always called me your all-knowing buddy, and I will continue my journey of education and self-growth. I can accomplish anything with you by my side.

Next, I dedicate this to my two amazing doctors who have helped me overcome a traumatic brain injury, seizures, and a stroke. Their care allowed me to finish this book. To my Neurologist, Dr. George Stergis, I appreciate everything you have fought for and dealt with getting me to this point. You always told me I was like a son to you, and I felt that level of care and dedication to my health care. To my Neurorehabilitation doctor, Dr. Gregory O'Shanick, thank you for always having confidence and faith that I was not defined by my brain injury and can overcome anything I set my mind to.

Cherry Blossom

Rose Bush

Virginia Bluebells

Henry is enjoying his community garden. It is springtime, the weather is warm, and the sun is shining. Henry loves the garden because he is able to see the butterflies flying and hear the birds chirping.

Henry loves to smell the sweet smells coming from the flowers. His favorite is the fragrant buds from the lavender plant. As Henry is smelling the lavender, he is greeted with not only a sweet smell but a buzzing honey bee.

"Oh no," says Henry as he jumps back. He remembers that honey bees have stingers and is afraid that being too close puts him in danger. Little does he know that his view of honey bees is about to change forever, because out from behind the lavender bush pops a honey bee wearing a crown.

Thinking to himself, he mumbles, "What could go wrong?" No sooner does "wrong" pass his lips than he starts to spin and shrink at an alarming rate. "What is happening to me," he yells out. Honey, still circling the lavender bush, says, "To show you all about honey bees, I have turned you into one!"

Henry, getting used to his new wings, flies to the nearest puddle of water and sees his reflection. "Oh no!" he exclaims, "What do I do now?" Honey looks at him and with a tilt of her crown, says, "Follow me, and I will teach you what I can."

Buzzing through the air, Honey leads Henry to a nearby newly opened lavender bud. Henry, still adapting to his new wings, struggles to keep up and finally joins her. Honey looks at Henry, "Now listen here, Henry, plants like lavender would not be possible without honey bees. We help them grow by carrying pollen from one plant to another. This is called pollination and without it, plants would struggle to grow."

"Hurry on now, " Honey says, "We have lots to see!" They take off and fly through rows of plants, dodging stems and flying past other insects who live in the garden.

Henry, new to being a honey bee, gets used to flying and loses his concentration. Bang! Henry feels a big push on his side as he is thrust to the right. This startles him until he looks up and realizes he almost ran into a large wooden frame with a small opening. Honey, who knocked Henry out of the way, exclaims, "What are you thinking? You almost ran into our home!"

Henry is blown away by the size and busyness of the hive. It is so large compared to him and Honey. Nothing could explain the large number of honey bees flying back and forth out of the hive opening.

Apple Blossoms

Honey, letting Henry regain himself, says, "Welcome Home! This is the hive!" Henry looks around and notices that not all bees look the same. He turns to Honey, "Why are the honey bees different sizes?" She answers, happy that he is taking an interest, "The honey bees are different sizes because they play different roles."

"I am the largest," states Honey. "I am the queen. I am responsible for providing the new honey bees and keeping the hive together. There is only one of me! Also, if I sting you, it is to protect myself, and it does not harm me."

Apple Blossoms

"The second-largest are the drones!" exclaims Honey. "They are responsible for providing new honey bees as well. There is more than one drone, but fewer than the worker bees. Drones do not have stingers and will never bother you, Henry."

"The smallest honey bees are the worker bees, " informs Honey. "They are responsible for picking our home, taking care of me, nursing the new honey bees, building and cleaning our home, and collecting the nectar and pollen from plants. This is the bee that you met before I showed up. Worker bees are the ones you see out in the wild that people are afraid of being stung by. Remember Henry, just like humans, honey bees only sting if they are threatened. So treat them with respect, and you will never have an issue with them."

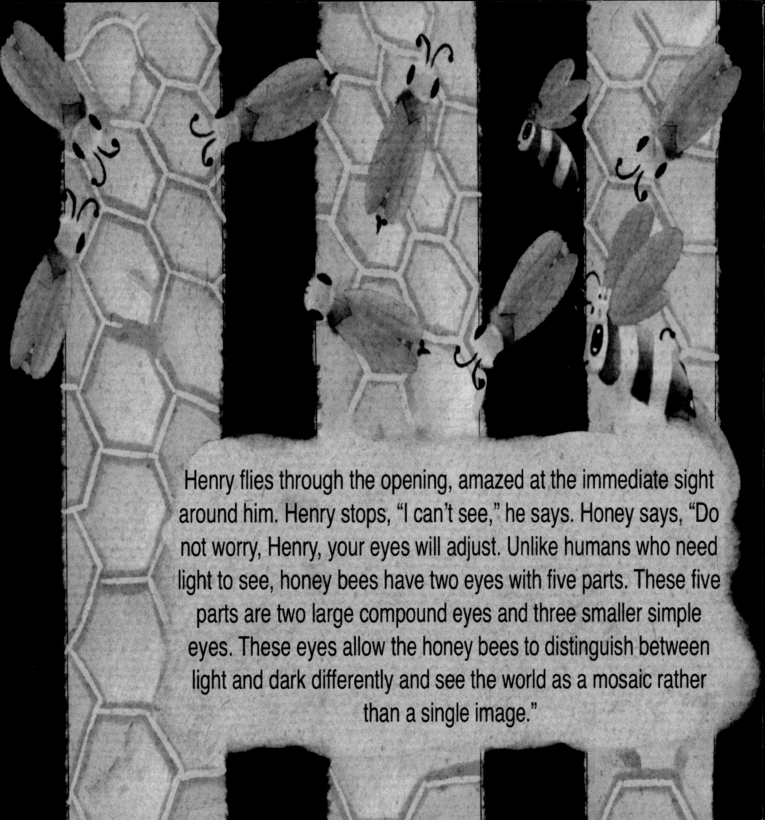

Henry flies through the opening, amazed at the immediate sight around him. Henry stops, "I can't see," he says. Honey says, "Do not worry, Henry, your eyes will adjust. Unlike humans who need light to see, honey bees have two eyes with five parts. These five parts are two large compound eyes and three smaller simple eyes. These eyes allow the honey bees to distinguish between light and dark differently and see the world as a mosaic rather than a single image."

As Henry's eyes start to adjust, a whole new world opens up for him. He watches in amazement as thousands of honey bees hustle around doing their jobs, the honey is locked in the honeycomb, and Honey takes her place on the honeycomb as the queen of the bees.

"Are you ready to learn about each job?" asks Honey. Henry, bewilderment in his eyes, utters a barely audible, "Yes." Honey starts to walk away as Henry rushes to catch up. "Quick, follow me," she says as she leads Henry to the worker bees who work as cleaners.

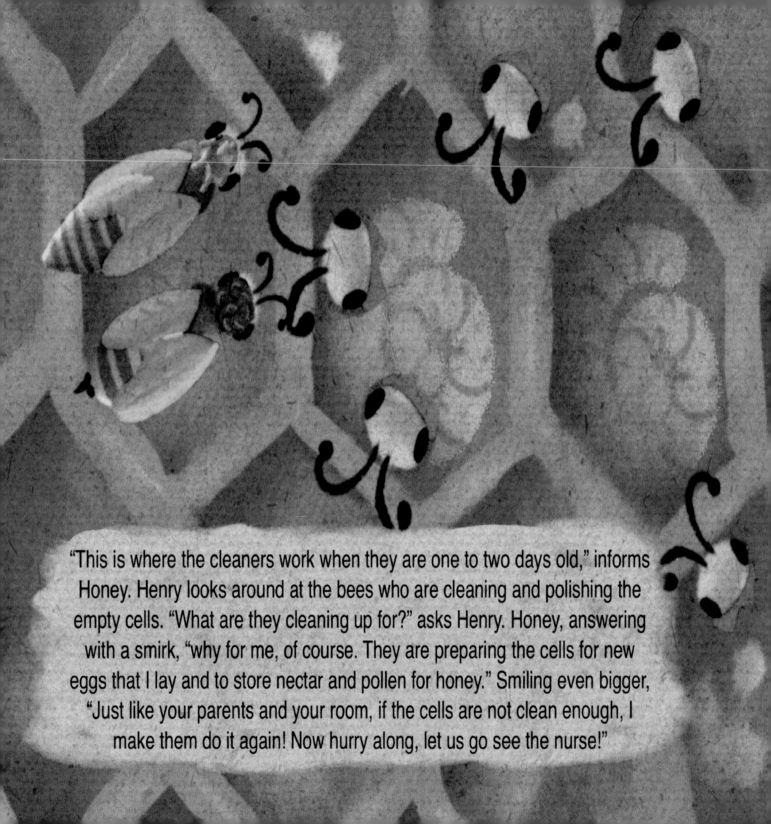

"This is where the cleaners work when they are one to two days old," informs Honey. Henry looks around at the bees who are cleaning and polishing the empty cells. "What are they cleaning up for?" asks Henry. Honey, answering with a smirk, "why for me, of course. They are preparing the cells for new eggs that I lay and to store nectar and pollen for honey." Smiling even bigger, "Just like your parents and your room, if the cells are not clean enough, I make them do it again! Now hurry along, let us go see the nurse!"

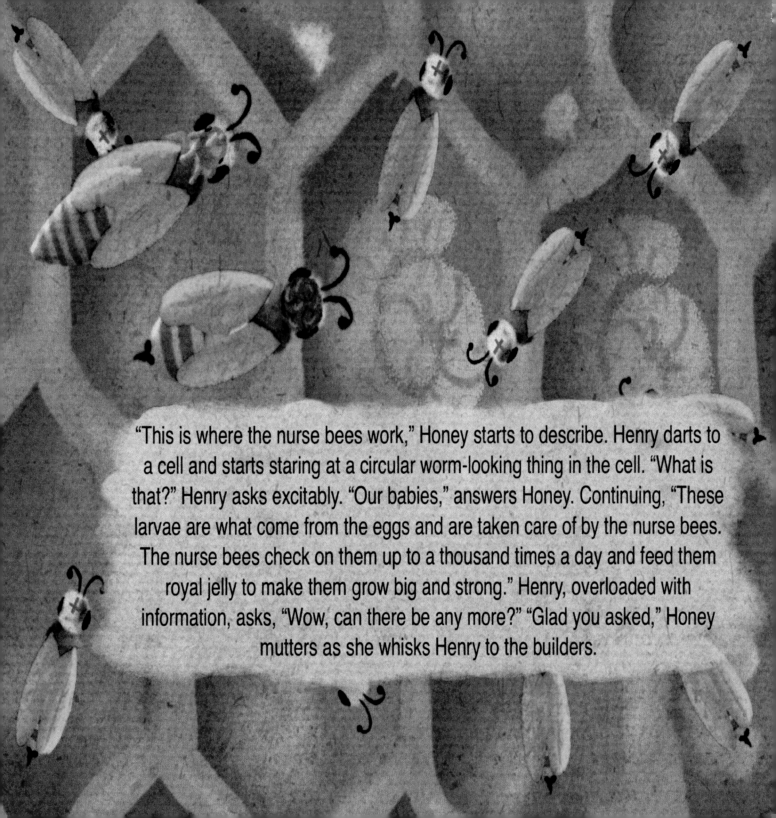

"This is where the nurse bees work," Honey starts to describe. Henry darts to a cell and starts staring at a circular worm-looking thing in the cell. "What is that?" Henry asks excitably. "Our babies," answers Honey. Continuing, "These larvae are what come from the eggs and are taken care of by the nurse bees. The nurse bees check on them up to a thousand times a day and feed them royal jelly to make them grow big and strong." Henry, overloaded with information, asks, "Wow, can there be any more?" "Glad you asked," Honey mutters as she whisks Henry to the builders.

Henry and Honey watch the bees move back and forth, making beeswax, building the cells that the larvae grow within, and the cleaners clean. "These are the builders. They are responsible for making the wax that builds the cells." Honey explains as Henry listens intently. She continues with, "The builders need large amounts of food to make these wax flakes, and they build them into honeycomb structures." "Wow!" exclaims Henry before stopping short. Looking worried, Henry states, " It is starting to get hot in here." Honey, leading the way, "Let us go see the temperature bees."

"Oh!" says Henry with a sigh of relief, "It is much cooler here." "These are the temperature control bees," says Honey. "They are responsible for cooling the hive in the spring and summer." "Well, what keeps it warm in the winter?" asked Henry. Honey, looking saddened, explains, "We cluster together to keep warm in the winter and we live off of honey stores we gathered in the spring and summer. Some bees may not make it through winter, so I lay eggs to replace anyone who does not make it." "This is so interesting, but I have a question." states Henry, "Who protects the hive?"

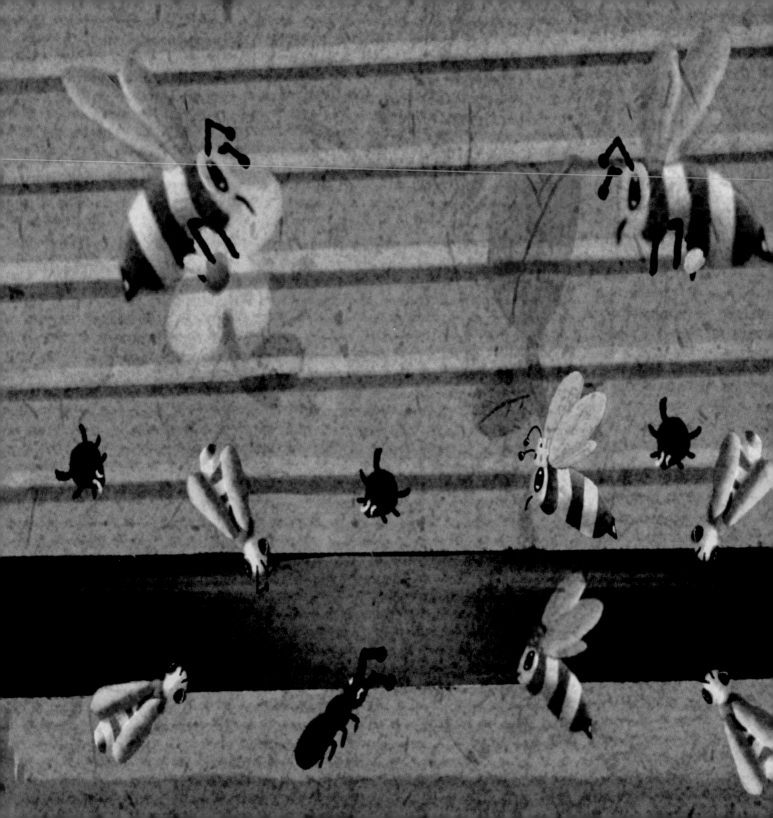

"I thought you would never ask," states Honey leading Henry back to the entrance to teach him about the last two jobs of the worker bees. "Now, I will teach you about the foragers and the guard bees," says Honey stopping to see if Henry is still with her. She continues, "These are the guard bees. Their last job before becoming foragers. They are responsible for keeping away bees from other hives, called robbers, and other pests that may try to get in the hive. Their role is vital to the survival of the hive itself." Wide-eyed as bees fly in with giant yellow balls of pollen around their back legs, Henry asks, "what are they?" Tipping her crown as a forager passes by, "Those are the foragers. They are responsible for getting pollen and nectar from the plants as you saw before this entire journey. They push the pollen to the pollen baskets on thier back legs. Plants would not grow without us, and we would not grow without them."

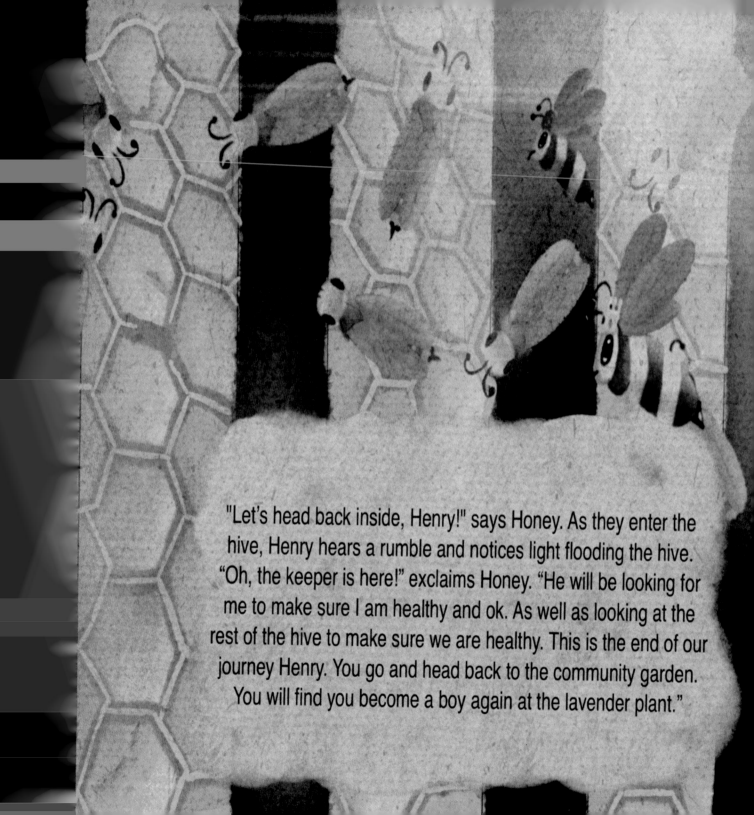

"Let's head back inside, Henry!" says Honey. As they enter the hive, Henry hears a rumble and notices light flooding the hive. "Oh, the keeper is here!" exclaims Honey. "He will be looking for me to make sure I am healthy and ok. As well as looking at the rest of the hive to make sure we are healthy. This is the end of our journey Henry. You go and head back to the community garden. You will find you become a boy again at the lavender plant."

Henry, flustered by the commotion and buzzing, flies past puffs of smoke. Taking a second to look over his shoulder, he mouths, "Thank you!" and continues on his journey past the lilies and lands on the bud of the lavender plant.

Without a moment to lose, Henry tries to rush the process of becoming a boy again by saying, "I want to be a boy again, I want to be a boy again." Before you know it, with a shining swirl of light and an immediate increase in size, Henry realizes he has become a boy again. After his experience, Henry vows to do his part to save the bees and become a beekeeper.